Edwardian Gardens

Edwardian Gardens

Anne Jennings

ENGLISH HERITAGE

IN ASSOCIATION WITH THE MUSEUM OF GARDEN HISTORY

Front cover: **Gertrude Jekyll at The Deanery, Sonning (Berks) c1901**

Back cover: **Photograph from the Museum of Garden History's collection, 1910**

Published by English Heritage, 23 Savile Row, London W1S 2ET
in association with the Museum of Garden History, Lambeth Palace Road,
London SE1 7LB

Copyright © English Heritage and Museum of Garden History

Anne Jennings is identified as the author of this work and asserts her moral
right to be acknowledged as copyright holder in the text.

First published 2005

ISBN 1 85074 905 1
Product code 50929

A CIP catalogue for this book is available from the British Library

Edited and brought to press by Adèle Campbell
Designed by Michael McMann
Technical editor Rowan Blaik
Printed by Bath Press

CONTENTS

Introduction

This book explores the background and styles of Edwardian gardens. It looks at how they developed from the colourful bedding displays and exotic planting schemes so beloved of the Victorians to be the hallmark of one of this country's most elegant ages. Large or small, the gardens of the Edwardian period were designed as places for relaxation, and many remain today as enduring reminders of this elegant period in history.

Although covering only some 30 years, the Edwardian period made a dramatic impact on British gardening. It is often considered to be a golden era during which the wealthy enjoyed a luxurious standard of living. Before the outbreak of the First World War labour was plentiful and cheap and teams of gardeners were employed to care for large gardens in the country. Meanwhile, in the fast growing suburbs, the middle classes were enjoying what was for many the first experience of home and garden ownership.

Throughout this book, a number of practical 'how-to' sections provide tips on creating Edwardian-style features for your own garden. Lists of flowering plants, shrubs and climbers popular with gardeners in the early 20th century provide ideas for planting that will evoke an Edwardian feel. The lists also give the availability of these plants, both as seeds and container-grown stock, in UK nurseries.

Postcard advertising a Royal Horticultural Society flower show, 1913

When Edward VII succeeded Queen Victoria in 1901 Britain was in the midst of a golden age. Victoria's reign had brought unprecedented change to all aspects of life in Britain and though the nation mourned her, Edward's accession was greeted with optimism. At the start of the 20th century one in four people in the world lived in the British Empire and for a few more years the nation maintained the enormous worldwide influence it had enjoyed under Victoria.

This was a time when the wealthy enjoyed financial security and teams of gardeners, essential for maintaining the herbaceous borders, kitchen gardens and yards of clipped hedges that were essential elements of the Edwardian country garden, were still relatively cheap to employ. Extravagant Ellen Willmott of Warley Place, Essex, was said to have over 80 men working in her garden, and even the hands-on Gertrude Jekyll employed 17 on her seven acres at Munstead Wood in Surrey.

Britain at this time was a hub for expanding global trade and the international movement of plants was easier and more reliable than ever before. British gardens had their own unique style but foreign influences were eagerly absorbed. Japanese gardens enjoyed a short period of popularity and plant-hunting expeditions to the Far East and the European Alps inspired interest in making rock gardens in Britain.

A photograph taken in the gardens at Pittachope, Scotland, and sent to friends of the sitter in 1909

At the same time, gardening was becoming an increasingly popular pastime for the growing urban middle classes, and Britain's expanding postal service and an ever-improving rail and road network gave them greater access to new plants and design ideas than ever before. Once foreign plants had

Alpine squill, Scilla bifolia, *was popular in Edwardian rock gardens*

Swing Hammock Chair with Awning.

No. 121 S.

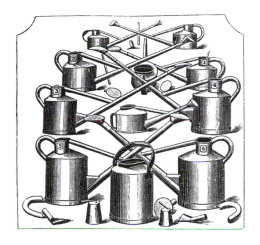

Watering cans and a hammock seat from William Woods & Son's 1909 catalogue

been introduced they quickly became available to the masses through nurserymen, who could now sell direct from their premises and by mail order. There was a massive expansion in the range of garden-related products available, with everything from rustic furniture and buildings to glass cloches, path edgings, thermometers, stoneware, machinery, hammocks, tools and much more, advertised in lavishly-illustrated catalogues.

Large-scale printing techniques made horticultural catalogues and books cheaper to produce and available to a wider market. Gardening magazines and periodicals published since the late 18th century remained popular, with new titles being added to the list: *Amateur Gardening* was published in 1884 and *Country Life* appeared in 1897, full of images and articles about some of the country's finest houses and gardens.

These publications were illustrated with line drawings, woodcuts and coloured botanical paintings. Beatrice Parsons and George Elwood became well known through these publications for their watercolours of garden scenes.

Black and white photography was used too, and thanks to the introduction of the box camera in 1888 an increasing number of personal photographs and commercially-produced postcards took garden themes and garden scenes to a wider audience. Today these provide a delightful insight into Edwardian life, their evocative images showing us not only what gardens looked like but how they were used and who owned and worked in them.

The outbreak of the First World War was to change everything, and the social and economic effects of the conflict were to impact on everyone's lives. Those who had previously enjoyed a privileged and luxurious lifestyle could no longer afford to make and maintain large country gardens and this golden age of gardening ended with the close of Edwardian period.

A rustic seat from William Woods & Son's 1909 catalogue

No. 206.
Rustic Tree Seat.
Artistic Design.   Strong and durable.   In hard rustic wood.
Price, **£7 10/-**

Edwardian country gardens are often thought to epitomise British garden-making at its best. Wonderful gardens drew house and land together in a perfect partnership of architecture and horticulture and it was this recognition of the relationship between plants and buildings that really dictated Edwardian garden style. But the trend began some 40 years earlier, in 1861, when artist, designer, writer and social reformer William Morris established the Arts and Crafts Movement.

William Morris and the Arts and Crafts Movement

The Arts and Crafts Movement rejected the mass production that had proliferated in Victorian Britain and celebrated traditional crafts and individual design. It brought together all kinds of skills, including book-binding, calligraphy, carpentry, pottery and embroidery, and with such a broad range of outlets and media it was natural for gardens and garden design to reflect its influence. Although plants and flowers had long inspired William Morris's work, it was not until his later years that he became interested in gardens and even then he was not known to be a practical gardener. Nevertheless, his name and that of the Arts and Crafts Movement are woven through the whole story of Edwardian garden design, which gathers together some of the greatest names in the horticulture and architecture of the time.

> ...[the garden] should by no means imitate either the wilfulness or wildness of nature...

The pergola at Hestercombe House, Somerset

Morris's home in Bexley Heath, The Red House, was designed by Arts and Crafts architect Philip Webb, who was also responsible for the gardens. Webb used medieval themes, much approved of by the Arts and Crafts cognoscenti, in the woven fences that separated each small garden from the next. Webb used white jasmine, roses and honeysuckle to grow up brick walls and lavender and rosemary to edge flower beds.

This method of using plants to soften formal lines and architectural structures is typical of Arts and Crafts garden design. Every opportunity was taken to combine hard and soft landscaping and plants became the softening 'flesh' around the 'bones' of the garden – the hard landscaping, which included terraces, paths, pools, summerhouses and pergolas. Planting often came right up to the house with wisteria, roses, clematis, honeysuckle and jasmine trained up walls, around windows and over doors. To integrate house and garden even further, herbs and other creeping plants were often introduced into paving and generous beds were made around the base of the house walls. These were planted with a mixture of flowering shrubs, perennials and annuals and in maturity the house would literally be clothed in plants.

> …[the garden] should by no means imitate either the wilfulness or wildness of nature, but should look like a thing never to be seen except near a house. It should in fact look like part of a house.

> *Making the Best of It*, William Morris lecture, 1879

William Morris, photographed by Frederick Hollyer in 1874

Any vertical surface, be it a wall or the upright post of a pergola, was seen as a support for climbing plants and even the rise of a step or the low face of a retaining wall would not escape adornment. Plants like Mexican daisy, *Erigeron karvinskianus* syn *Erigeron mucranatus* 'Profusion', grew along steps, along with lavenders, thymes and other herbs.

Formal ponds contained water lilies, flowering shrubs billowed over the back of stone or wooden benches and through balustrades, and plants cascaded down the face of rockeries. The newly laid-out garden was a blank canvas waiting to be filled with the colour, texture, form and pattern provided by plants, in true Arts and Crafts style.

The style influenced and inspired many great architects of the period, such as Charles Voysey, who were to build some of the country's most beautiful houses that are still much admired today. Some, like Sir Reginald Blomfield, became as heavily

Details of seats and terracing by Arts and Crafts designer
Charles Ashbee, early 1900s

involved in the design of the gardens as they were with the house and the work of Sir Edwin Lutyens was to have lasting impact on gardens of the period, due to his working partnership with the plantswoman Gertrude Jekyll.

Hard landscaping in the Arts and Crafts garden reflected the Movement's celebration of traditional crafts and the beauty of individual design. The materials that created such a strong link between house and garden were, wherever possible, local to the area. Great attention was paid to details of the stonework;

Beautiful stone and brickwork surround the pool on the west side of Goddards, Surrey, a Lutyens house with garden by Jekyll

in steps, pools and terraces for example. The designs too were chosen to reflect local tradition and were executed with great care; such as regularly-laid stone slabs accented with tile detail, or bricks set in basket-weave or herringbone patterns. For coastal gardens, stones and pebbles might be set into cement to create textured and patterned surfaces evocative of the seashore. However simple the concept, the effects were frequently stunning and married house, garden and their setting beautifully.

These gardens had a sense of mystery about them; of hidden spaces and outdoor rooms. Garden designers delighted in using changes of level, to make strong architectural statements and to enhance the sense of journey through the various

The west rill in the gardens of Hestercombe House, Somerset

elements of the garden. Elaborate steps were popular – right-angled or circular styles, reducing in width towards the top, were common. Shallow risers and broad treads were often used as they made for a comfortable journey, and a slight overhang on each tread added pleasing detail as well as a light shadow to accentuate the change of level. If the steps could lead to a wooden or iron gate providing an intriguing view to the next level, then all the better. Retaining walls next to the steps provided more planting opportunities: below, on top and into the face of the wall.

Water was an important element in Edwardian gardens and was used in various ways. Formal geometric pools were built from materials similar or complementary to those used in the paths and walkways, and could be simple water-lily reservoirs or might hold a central statue or fountain. Changes in level provided opportunities to create cascades, but perhaps the most elegant Edwardian water feature was the rill. These shallow, narrow canals were usually edged in stone or brick and some, like the beautiful examples at Hestercombe in Somerset, and Coleton Fishacre in Devon, incorporated tiny, stone-edged pools, fed by the main route.

A classic feature of Edwardian gardens was to divide the outdoor space into smaller rooms. This was generally achieved with yew hedges, like those planted by Lawrence Johnston at

Hidcote Manor in Gloucestershire. Other features included low hedges of box to delineate beds, and beech, lime and hornbeam were trained into 'pleached' screens that further divided the garden.

Water tanks, sun dials, urns, well-heads and similar features in an Arts and Crafts garden were often Gothic or Italianate in style, and the materials they were made from were also chosen with care, with lead or stone considered most suitable for English gardens.

> *The busts of the Caesars and other ornaments*
> *and sculptures in white marble are not quite at*
> *home in our gardens…we have more suitable*
> *material in our home quarries…There can*
> *scarcely be any doubt that the happiest material*
> *for our garden sculpture and ornament is*
> *lead…the surface of the metal, with age and*
> *exposure, acquires a patina of silvery grey that*
> *harmonizes well with our garden evergreens.*
>
> Garden Ornament **by Gertrude Jekyll, 1918**

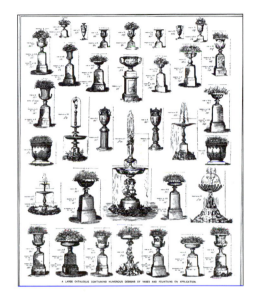

A selection of garden ornaments from William Woods and Son's catalogue, 1909

Opposite: **Mexican daisy, Erigeron karvinskianus**

create a pleached screen

8 feet – 2.4 metres

Pleached trees create an effective and space-economic screen or divider for your garden. 'Pleaching' is the practice of training young trees to grow to roughly 1.8m high before allowing any side branches to develop. The side branches are then trained along and tied onto horizontal wires, to create a flat screen. Any forward growth has to be removed as soon as it appears. This technique was traditionally used in large country gardens but it can be adapted to smaller sites.

Traditional trees for pleaching are hornbeam, beach, lime and holly, but in smaller gardens you could use pyracantha, arbutus or large evergreen shrubs like photinia or cotoneaster.

First mark out the length of your screen, allowing a distance of approximately 2.4m (8') between each tree. The first tree should be planted 1.2m (4') from the start of the screen and the last one the same distance from the end. If you are planting an avenue, make sure the trees are directly opposite each other.

A framework will be needed to support the trees while they are young. Drive a strong timber post roughly 0.6–0.9m (2–3') into the ground for each tree: the post should be as high as the finished screen. A post will also be needed at each end of the screen (round timber will look better than square). On exposed sites the posts may need to be set in concrete. Next fix either timber lathes or taut wire horizontally between each post. Starting at the top, position the horizontals approximately 0.3m (1') apart, down to the lowest point of the screen.

Plant your trees midway between the posts, digging a large hole and incorporating plenty of organic matter into the soil. On exposed sites you may need a stake against each tree trunk. Any young branches that appear low down the trunk or grow out at right angles from it need to be removed immediately. Tie in any suitable branches to the wires with string, laying them as near horizontal as possible. If the main stem or 'leader' is too high, bend it onto the top horizontal.

Each winter, continue to train and tie the growth horizontally and remove any unusable wood. Prune the end of all growths by a few centimetres to encourage more shoots further down the stem. When the screen is mature you will be able to cut it with shears, as you would a hedge.

Italianate influence

Many Arts and Crafts practitioners were inspired by classic Italian Renaissance gardens, which relied as much on architecture as plants for their beauty. Author George Sitwell created an Italianate garden at Renishaw Hall, his family home in Derbyshire. Architects Inigo Triggs and Harold Peto combined their love of Arts and Crafts and Italian Renaissance design: Peto's work can be seen around his home at Iford Manor near Bradford-on-Avon and at Easton Lodge in Essex, where he redesigned the gardens for Daisy, Countess of Warwick in 1902.

The gardens at Iford Manor in 1907

Another author, American-born Edith Wharton (1861–1937), was a lifelong gardener and lover of all things Italian; two passions she combined in her book *Italian Villas and their Gardens* published in 1904. She adored the combination of Italianate architecture with both formal and informal planting and her work was of great influence to the wealthier classes:

> …*to enjoy and appreciate the Italian garden-craft one must always bear in mind that it is independent of floriculture. The Italian garden does not exist for flowers; its flowers exist for it…*
> *This is no doubt partly explained by the difficulty of cultivating any but spring flowers in so hot and dry a climate, and the result has been a wonderful development of the more permanent effects to be obtained from three other factors in garden composition – marble, water and perennial verdure…*

Italian Villas and Their Gardens by Edith Wharton, 1904

Italian garden style, in common with Arts and Crafts designs, focused on creating a strong relationship between house and garden, with the architecture of one complementing and enhancing the other. 'Soft' architectural lines were created with holly and laurel walks and bowling-green-quality lawns.

But Edith Wharton recognised that in many respects the Italian garden could not be recreated in other countries, saying 'some critics have thence inferred that the Italian garden is, so to speak, *untranslatable*'.

> *...a marble sarcophagus and a dozen twisted columns will not make an Italian garden; but a piece of ground laid out and planted on the principles of the old garden-craft will be, not indeed an Italian garden in the literal sense, but, what is far better, a garden as well adapted to its surroundings as were the models which inspired it.*
>
> **Italian Villas and Their Gardens by Edith Wharton, 1904**

Gertrude Jekyll, one of the best-known Edwardian gardeners, shared Edith Wharton's love of Italianate garden design. As an artist she understood the influences that had for so long inspired their creation:

> *When we remember the conditions under which the great gardens of Italy came into being, it is no longer a matter of wonder that they should stand out as examples of excellence, both in general design and in finished detail. For they were made at a time when there was that extraordinary*

The 'Stratton Design' sundial from the catalogue of JP White and Sons of Bond Street, London

Norah Lindsay, etching of a drawing probably by Marion, Duchess of Rutland

Norah Lindsay (1876–1948), a great romantic, socialite and garden advisor to the upper classes, incorporated elements of a traditional English garden, the romance of a 'wild' garden and elements of Italian architecture into the landscape at the Manor House at Sutton Courtenay in Oxfordshire. Though she favoured rustic poles over ornate brick pergolas for supporting roses, her introduction of formal pools and a loggia next to the house was influenced by her love of Italy. She once said of herself: 'I would have been a much lesser gardener had I not worshipped at the crumbling shrines of the ancient gods of Florence and Rome'.

William Robinson (1838–1935) was one of the most important horticultural figures of the time. His career spanned the Victorian and Edwardian eras and he spent most of it rebelling against formal Victorian planting and promoting 'naturalistic' styles and 'wild' gardening. He was particularly influential because of his prolific writing. Robinson founded *The Garden* magazine, which was in print from 1871 to 1927, and published *Gardening Illustrated* for the wealthier middle classes from 1879. His many books included *The English Flower Garden* (1883). Robinson's own work and writing was to inspire a whole new generation of gardeners, including the influential Gertrude Jekyll who adopted many of his planting ideas.

A long trip to France in the summer of 1867 provided Robinson with inspiration, when he saw bedding schemes destroyed by inclement weather and at the same time noticed how the Parisians had adapted tropical planting, using foliage plants that were more tolerant of wind, rain and cool temperatures than exotic flowering plants. He advocated a similar approach on his return to Britain, planting in natural-looking groups but substituting tender plants with hardy specimens. Robinson was passionate about his ideas and became an outspoken and opinionated gardener, instructing, persuading and bullying his readers into adopting his planting ideas. Topiary, formal hedges, geometric designs, mass carpets

...throwing aside all grace of form and loveliness of bloom, was indeed a dismal mistake...

Nasturtium, Tropaeolum majus, *suited Robinson's informal garden style*

of coloured bedding and the seasonal planting of exotics were all to be abandoned, he argued, on economic and practical, as well as aesthetic, grounds.

Robinson often used the Armenian grape hyacinth, Muscari armeniacum

> *To make a flower-bed to imitate a bad carpet, and by throwing aside all grace of form and loveliness of bloom, was indeed a dismal mistake … Useless, planting out in midsummer when half the flower charms of the year are past; misuse of the glass-houses which might grow welcome food in spring…*
>
> The English Flower Garden by William Robinson, 1883

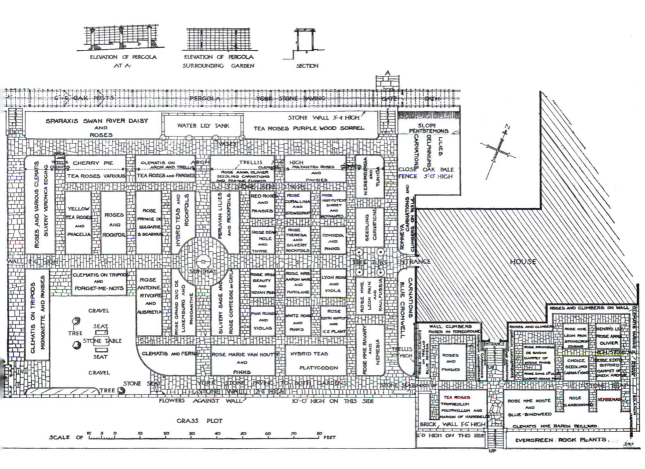

The flower garden plan at Gravetye.

A plan of William Robinson's garden at Gravetye

It is often assumed that William Robinson favoured only native plants in his 'wild' gardens but this was not the case; he grew many foreign plants at Gravetye Manor, his Surrey home. In simple terms, it was the use of hardy plants with an emphasis on a 'natural' planting style that inspired his passion and creativity. His theories complement the environmentally-aware approach that is encouraged today; to use plants that will thrive naturally in the local environment, without the need for additional irrigation, 'alien' soil or winter protection. He expands on this theme in *The English Flower Garden*:

> *In the cultivation of hardy plants and especially in wild gardening the important thing is to find out what things really do in the soil, without which much good way cannot be made. Many people make errors in planting things that are tender in our country and very often fail in consequence; but apart from such risky planting perfectly hardy plants may disappear owing to some dislike of the soil...what may be done with any good result in the wild garden cannot be determined beforehand but must depend on the nature of the soil and other circumstances which can only be known to those who study the ground.*

Although he had trained and worked as a professional gardener, Robinson was 47 when he bought Gravetye in 1885 and at last had a garden of his own. Property ownership perhaps clarified for him the need to create a certain formality

around the house, where he laid out terraces, pergolas and formal shaped beds.

Farther from the house Robinson planted trees, shrubs, perennials and bulbs to develop the 'wild' garden that he loved. His selection of flowering shrubs included specimens from New Zealand, America, Siberia and China, with escallonia, mahonia, cornus, rhododendron and hydrangea among his favourites. The Crimean pine, Cedar of Lebanon and American hickories were among thousands of non-native trees he planted. He recommended the cultivation of narcissi, anemones, snowdrops and bluebells, planted in natural groups beneath trees.

> *The term 'Wild Garden' is applied to the placing of perfectly hardy exotic plants in places where they will take care of themselves. It has nothing to do with the 'wilderness', though it may be carried out in it…What it does mean is best explained by the winter Aconite flowering under a grove of naked trees in February; by the Snowflake abundant in meadows by the Thames…*

The English Flower Garden

Opposite: **Foxtail lilies, engraved from a photograph for** The English Flower Garden

create Robinson-style 'living edges' and 'wild' planting

Living edges

William Robinson agreed that box had a place in the garden, but he objected to the 'wasteful work' of clipping 'many miles of box edging'. He suggested a combination of stone and alpine or dwarf plants for the front of a flower border, to create a soft structure that required much less maintenance than box.

To create a living edge, first set broken stone slabs vertically at edge of the bed (or between the bed and the path) to create a roughly level, but rugged, raised edge about 125mm (4") high.

Next choose your plants. For sunny borders, use babys' breath, *Gypsophila repens*, dwarf lavender, a pink such as *Dianthus plumaria*, aubretia, thyme and forms of saxifrage. In shady, cooler sites plant dwarf campanulas, viola, dwarf hardy geraniums or hepatica. Position the plants in a row immediately behind the slabs, so they can grow up and over the edge to soften it.

As an alternative to a stone edge, Robinson suggested clipped ivy for the shade (try *Hedera helix* 'Ivalace' for a modern substitute) or clipped rosemary for sunny areas, though these would not necessarily result in less clipping than box!

These plant 'recipes' give an idea of the combinations and groupings that William Robinson used in his 'wild' garden. They can be adapted to the scale of your planting scheme.

Wild planting – naturalised snowdrops

The simplest forms of snowdrop, *Galanthus nivalis*, self-seeds most efficiently so avoid double flowers and modern hybrids.

Buy snowdrops in spring when they are 'in the green' (after flowering) as dry bulbs can be unreliable. Many suppliers sell clumps of snowdrops that have been dug up after flowering, and you can often buy these through gardening magazines.

Try to find a site where the soil is deep and moist in winter and spring, as snowdrops thrive in these conditions (though they do require a dry period when the bulbs are dormant in summer).

Plant the snowdrops in natural-looking groups; they will self-seed, enhancing the 'wilderness' effect. Always wait until the leaves have turned brown before mowing, to ensure the bulb is 'fed' for the following season.

Other 'Robinson' bulbs that could be planted in this way are *Narcissus poeticus, Cyclamen hederifolium* and, for warm, light soil, the winter aconite, *Eranthis hyemalis*.

Gertrude Jekyll

Gertrude Jekyll (1843–1932) was a prolific garden writer and her books and magazine articles still inspire today's gardeners. It is as a plantswoman that she is most famous, however, and her unique planting style, influenced by William Robinson's ideas, clearly demonstrated an artist's use of colour, texture and form. Her work with the much younger architect, Edwin Lutyens, resulted in the creation of some of the most beautiful country gardens of the period.

Jekyll was born into the upper middle class in London in 1843, and when the family moved to Guildford four years later she fell in love with the Surrey countryside and learnt much about its native wild flowers. She trained at the School of Art in South Kensington and became a successful artist and craftswoman, working with a variety of media including embroidery, metalwork, woodwork and photography, in the spirit of the Arts and Crafts Movement. Alongside these artistic achievements Jekyll developed her interest in gardening, and when deteriorating eyesight cut short her other pursuits she diverted her talents into horticulture. She was a prolific and influential writer of gardening books and magazine articles, including contributing to William Robinson's publications.

Munstead Wood seen from the old annual garden

Soon after her decision to focus on gardening, when she was almost 50 years old, Gertrude Jekyll met 22-year-old Edwin Lutyens. He was a gentle, talented young man who loved traditional architecture and local crafts, and was again inspired by Arts and Crafts ideals. A friendship developed between the two and in 1896 Lutyens began work designing a home for Jekyll at Munstead Wood in Surrey. Their combined skills created a beautiful house that blended perfectly into the landscape and setting. This was to be the beginning of a remarkable partnership, with Lutyens earning commissions initially in and around Surrey, but later far and wide, and Jekyll providing plans and plants for the garden. In the early days she

The Early bulbous iris, Iris reticulata, *was often used by Jekyll*

would visit the sites but in later years provided planting plans and instructions by letter, never seeing her clients' gardens at all.

Classically, a Jekyll/Lutyens garden retained the expected formality near the house, where stone terraces, intricate steps, formal ponds and box-edged borders united house and garden. Away from the house were woodland or wild gardens, with perhaps a spring garden, cottage garden, or a kitchen garden. Jekyll loved the idea of simple plants cascading out of gaps in an old or purpose-built wall:

> It should be contrived either in connection with some old walls or, failing these, with some walls or wall-like structures built on purpose. These walls would shock the builder, but would delight a good gardener, for they would present just those conditions most esteemed by wall-loving plants, of crumbling masonry built of half-formed or half-rotting stones, and of loose joints made to receive rather than to repel every drop of welcome rain…
>
> *Home and Garden*, Gertrude Jekyll, 1900

Her planting schemes were carefully planned and she applied a complex set of rules to the use of colour, which translated as beautiful and seemingly simple combinations. One of her most innovative and influential ideas was the use of large swathes of plants to create clouds of colour. Jekyll introduced dramatic herbaceous borders into many of her clients' gardens, though none were as experimental as those at Munstead where a team of gardeners was employed to maintain extensive beds. Some of these extended to 200 feet long and 14 feet wide, and flowered from July until October. Plants required staking and dead-heading, and other techniques were used to disguise the unattractive remains of

Border at Munstead Wood, taken in 1907

FERTILO

HARVEY'S UNIVERSAL FERTILIZER

A Stimulating Food for all Plants

Invigorating
Lasting
Safe
Clean
Cheap

Testimonials
Press
Opinions
on
other side.

At Shrewsbury
GREAT SHOW 1904
One Exhibitor WON
·15· PRIZES
by using
FERTILO

The Fertilizer for the
AMATEUR and
the **PROFESSIONAL GARDENER**.

Manufacturers:
J. P. HARVEY & CO.,
KIDDERMINSTER.

BLAKE & MACKENZIE, LIVERPOOL.

early flowering specimens; scrambling climbers were teased through borders and container-grown hardy, half-hardy and tender plants were introduced throughout the season to extend interest. In *Colour in the Flower Garden* (1908) Jekyll explained the complex planning behind the apparently simple effects in her borders:

> *Even when a flower border is devoted to a special season, as mine is from mid-July to October, it cannot be kept fully furnished without resorting to various contrivances…Delphiniums, which are indispensable for July, leave bare stems with quickly yellowing leafage when the flowers are over. We plant behind them the white Everlasting Pea and again behind that Clematis Jackmannii. When the Delphiniums are over, the rapidly forming seed pods are removed, the stems are cut down to just the right height, and the white peas are trained over them. When the Peas go out of bloom in the middle of August, the Clematis is brought over…..It is not easy at all. It has taken me half a lifetime merely to find out what is best worth doing, and a good slice out of another half to puzzle out the way of doing it.*

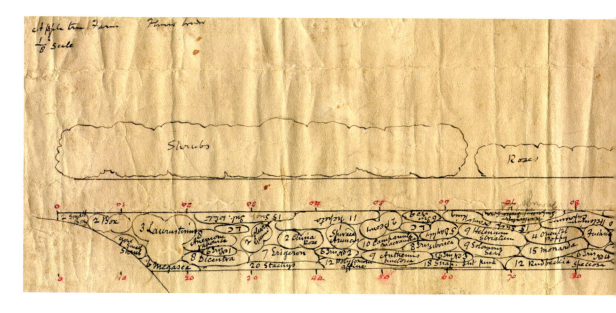

Gertrude Jekyll's planting plan for a border at the
Hertfordshire garden of conductor Sir Henry Wood

Jekyll's woodland gardens were also designed to create the feeling of a natural environment; harmonious and 'natural' scenes created with her trademark technical use of colour combined with skilfully-contoured paths and carefully grouped plants and trees. Jekyll's artistic training encouraged her to exaggerate the impact of sunlight, especially in the woodland where transient theatrical effects could be created – groups of white foxgloves illuminated by a shaft of sunlight for example or, as used at Munstead, a mass of pink, white and rose-flowered rhododendrons planted around the white trunk of a birch tree.

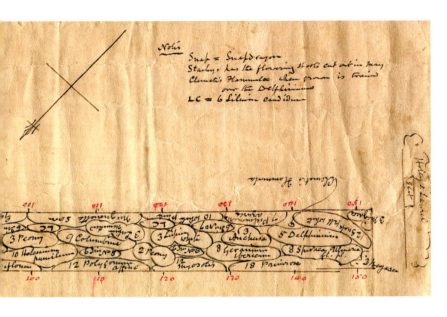

From this same walk in June, looking westward
through the Birch stems, the value of the careful
colour-scheme of the Rhododendrons is truly felt.
They are about a hundred yards away, and their
mass is broken by the groups of intervening tree
trunks, but their brightness is all the more
apparent seen from under the nearer roofing
mass of tree-top, and the yellowing light makes
the intended colour-effect still more successful by
throwing its warm tone over the whole.

Colour in the Flower Garden by Gertrude Jekyll, 1908

create Jekyll-style colour-themed planting

As well as moving through different colours within a single border, Gertrude Jekyll also planted single-colour themed beds, with one colour dominating but supported by other shades and tones. One of the best examples of this type is the grey border, where grey and silver foliaged plants provide a backdrop to other flowering plants. Adapt the number and repetition of plants to suit the size of your border.

The best location is a sunny, open site with good, well-drained soil. Use foliage shrubs and woody plants for the grey 'backbone' to the scheme, for example lamb's ears, *Stachys lanata*, cotton lavender, *Santolina chamaecyparrissus* and wormwood *Artemesia ludoviciana*.

Plant these in key positions within the border as shown on the example opposite.

Choose other plants with grey or silver in their foliage to go in and around the grey-leaved plants, for example Miss Wilmott's Ghost, *Eryngium giganteum* and the globe thistle *Echinops ritro*.

Finally, select some flowering plants that complement the grey theme; Gertrude Jekyll used hollyhocks, *alcea rosaea*, snapdragons, *antirrhinum* and baby's breath, *gypsophilia repens*.

Timber posts or other upright supports can be used within the scheme to support climbing plants whose blooms complement the colours of your scheme – pink or white clematis or roses would be good.

If you need a backdrop to the planting, choose larger plants that reflect the grey theme: variegated *Pittosporum*, *Buddleia alternifolia* or *Elaeagnus angustifolia* would be perfect.

Globe thistle, Echinops ritro

Urban gardens of the middle class

In the city and suburbs, far from the world inhabited by Morris, Robinson and Jekyll, gardening was an equally fashionable pastime, but in many ways it had its own horticultural style and culture quite distinct from that found in the country.

A high demand for homes in the first decade of the 20th century generated enormous building programmes and large middle-class estates appeared on the outskirts of towns and cities. For the first time, each house had its own back garden with larger houses having space at the front too. A completely new class of garden owner was created and a new literature appeared to cater for them.

The Back Garden Beautiful, by Harry Havart, was aimed at the lower-middle class and instructed the novice gardener on the design, construction, planting and maintenance of his plot. The book included simple designs to copy, ranging from 'an effective, if somewhat simple, garden arrangement' to 'something out of the ordinary'. Each incorporated a central lawn with borders enclosing the garden on three sides and a gravel path running down the fourth, with a specific position detailed for the 'cylindrical galvanised dustbin which most municipal authorities insist upon…one of those evils which have to be endured'. Some designs included a greenhouse and other elaborations such as rustic arches, ornamental

…street urchins are such arrant lovers of other people's flowers…

A small back garden in Bristol, 1910

43

stone vases and trellis screens. Havart's suggestions for a 'Quick Result Garden', ideal for tenants of a 'migratory character', were based on hardy annuals and perennials, such as foxgloves, hollyhocks, larkspur, lupins and candy tuft; an autumn-flowering equivalent would include Japanese anemones, red-hot pokers and Michaelmas daisies.

Hollyhocks were popular in urban gardens; this one is **Alcea tourinensis**

[This book] was written with the idea of appealing to those people who, for perhaps the first time in their lives, find themselves happy in the tenancy or possession of a small house with a tiny garden attached thereto. Tens of thousands of such homes spring up every year in the suburbs of London and other great cities…..as fine old houses are pulled down and the sites and grounds developed for building purposes….

The Back Garden Beautiful by Harry Havart, 1909 and 1912

New householders slightly higher up the social scale needed more help and advice on running their homes than their lower middle classes contemporaries. They had bigger houses, often employed staff and had demanding social commitments. Their homes were private havens, symbols of wealth and became a means of demonstrating success and status.

Even the smallest front gardens could be enhanced with a profusion of flowers, c1905

A house with a front garden, for example, distinguished its owner from the lower classes, whose front door often opened immediately onto the pavement. Hedges separated one upper-middle-class property from the next, and the owners were screened from the road and passing pedestrians by walls, railings, gates or hedges that in many ways emulated the country homes of the wealthy.

Within these boundaries, however, as garden writer A C Curtis explained, there was very little scope for anything other than a simple and practical design for the front garden:

> *In the plan of front gardens very little originality is possible, the conditions are fixed, and near London the street urchins are such arrant lovers of other people's flowers. There is depth varying in different gardens of from fifteen to thirty feet, and through this little scrap of ground way must be made both to the back and front entrances. Hence, two paths, a belt of shrubs to form a screen between the house and road, and also between the house and 'next door' and some well-kept grass, form, almost inevitably, the basis of the composition.*

> *The Small Garden Beautiful*, 1906

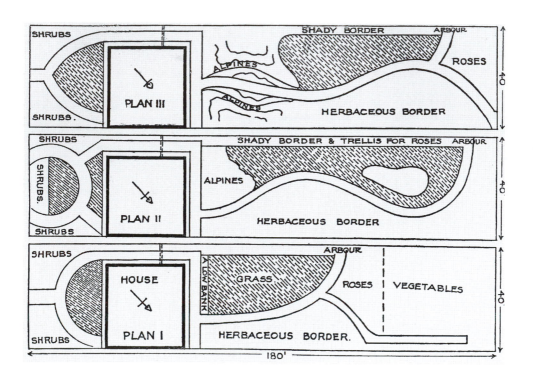

Three of Curtis's designs for back gardens from **The Small Garden Beautiful**

Curtis goes on to explain that the front gate of a semi-detached house should not be directly opposite the door, but should approach it from an angle 'which does not come too easily within view of the dear old Misses Prigg, who take such a keen interest in all their neighbours' doings.' Narrow borders running around the house were to be planted with climbing plants surrounded by bright annuals mixed with violas and bulbs. A good architectural or foliage plan was often planted within the lawn and Curtis suggested Pampas grass, acanthus,

Berberis stenophylla or *Magnolia stellata*, an idea copied for decades afterwards.

Curtis advised on back gardens too, which were larger than those dealt with by Havart and could extend up to a quarter of an acre. In *The Small Garden Beautiful* Curtis encouraged his readers to create distinct areas within the site; a rock garden, water garden, a small kitchen garden and herbaceous borders. He provided design suggestions for formal and informal gardens, the formal gardens having more geometric lines with sections separated into 'rooms' by trellis screens and planting, and the less formal effects created with sweeping lines and organically-shaped borders and lawns.

In bad weather homeowners could enjoy their garden through French doors or, if their circumstances allowed, from a conservatory. Greenhouses and conservatories became increasingly popular and there were a large number of practical gardening books and encyclopaedias encouraging homeowners to grow exotic and tender plants. The range of plants expanded each year: orchids, coleus, cineraria, oleander and freesia were grown as pot plants and tender climbers like bougainvillea, abutilon, hoya and plumbago were planted in large containers or a soil border.

Enjoying the greenhouse in the early 20th century

Edwardians in their gardens

Edwardians took full advantage of the art of photography to record their homes and gardens. Many of their photos were sent to friends as postcards. This selection is from the Museum of Garden History's collection.

Clockwise from top left: 'Mr Luty' (in the background) in Yorkshire, 1907; c1910; c1905; Aston, Birmingham, c1910

Edwardians in their gardens

Top: *Patients gardening at Mount Vernon Hospital, Northwood, Middlesex c1915*
Below: *family group, 1904*

In overcrowded and polluted cities the number of public parks was growing, and the elaborate and colourful bedding schemes so despised by William Robinson became increasingly sophisticated. Local authorities considered it a matter of civic pride to plant as colourfully and imaginatively as possible throughout the summer months and, not content with patterned beds, constructed ambitious three-dimensional bedding that could be as elaborate as fully-working floral clocks. Shrubs failed to thrive in the polluted cities but bedding plants maintained a healthy, colourful display for several months, after which all the plants were ripped out before they succumbed to disease and fatigue.

The Italian Gardens at Saltburn dated 1907

Windsor,
Alexandra Gardens.

The parks were sources of inspiration for town dwellers as well as places for relaxation and recreation. Unconcerned with sophisticated debates about 'naturalistic' versus exotic planting schemes, the lower-middle classes sought ideas from the local park displays. Garden writer Walter Wright criticised local authorities for failing to inspire their visitors with more progressive ideas:

> The average suburban gardener has had to go for practical hints to the public parks, and these places have either been dragged along at snail's pace in the rear of garden improvement, or developed a flamboyant and bewildering style out of all proportion to the needs of the vast majority of people who frequent them. In these circumstances it is no cause for surprise that the suburbanist has accomplished so little, indeed the wonder is he has done so much.
>
> **The New Gardening, 1912**

Opposite: **Alexandra Gardens, Windsor, 1907**

Opposite, below: **The Carpet Gardens in Hesketh Park, Southport, c 1905**

The Garden City Movement

A growing concern about the number of people squeezed into the cities and the unhealthy environments created by industrial growth inspired an innovative solution: the Garden City Movement. First proposed by Sir Ebenezer Howard, the movement planned to tackle this problem by building new communities in beautiful environments, where people could both live and work in a rural setting. In *Garden Cities of Tomorrow* (1902) Howard explained his philosophy: 'by so laying out a Garden City that, as it grows, the free gifts of Nature – fresh air, sunlight, breathing room and playing room – shall be still retained in all needed abundance'.

The idea grasped the imagination of many, including supporters of the Arts and Crafts Movement and the Pre-Raphaelite Brotherhood of artists. Members of both organisations were involved in the creation and administration of the first Garden City in 1902 – Letchworth in Hertfordshire – where low-density building, avenues of trees and country greens surrounded by cottages complemented the rural theme. As well as enjoying communal gardens, most garden city residents had both a private front and back garden.

In Hampstead Garden Suburb, where homes were designed by Edwin Lutyens, only eight houses were built to an acre of land. Gardens had hedges or trellis-work boundaries and

Sir Ebenezer Howard, originator of the Garden City concept

'where possible, a colour scheme with the hedges.' As might be expected, however, once the residents were established in their new homes they began to impose a certain individuality on their gardens, a development that worried Walter Wright when he observed it in Letchworth: 'The inhabitants have not the communal spirit. Each concerns himself with the management of his own plot, without regard to the city as a whole.' Returning to his theme of using parks to inspire the design of private gardens, he suggested that fine public gardens should be made in the garden cities to inspire the new residents and provide harmony between public and private horticulture.

Back gardens at Letchworth Garden City, Hertfordshire

There are many women who made their own remarkable impact on British gardening during the Edwardian period. Opportunities arose for young ladies to enter the world of professional gardening by training at one of the several women's horticultural colleges that opened from the 1890s onwards.

Frances Evelyn, 'Daisy' Countess of Warwick, not only created the gardens at Easton Lodge but also established one of the first women's colleges. Unusually for a woman of her class, Daisy became a socialist and for many years was committed to encouraging young, educated women to train in horticulture and agriculture. Her concern for the 'one million surplus of women' and worries about rising unemployment figures inspired her to found the college, where women could be equipped with the skills to become financially independent.

> The gentlewomen of today are the daughters of an alert and self-reliant age, in which marriage is no longer the simple solution of every girl's life; in which strikes and speculations wreck fortunes every day. Portionless, or next to portionless, unmarried women of gentle birth and breeding find themselves face to face with the necessity of making money; some in order to keep the wolf from the doors, others towards supplementing a meagre income.
>
> *Lady's Realm*, November 1896

Daisy's college was established near Reading in 1898 but it quickly outgrew the premises and in 1903 it moved to a site near to the Countess' family seat, Warwick Castle. Soon after the move, Daisy relinquished involvement with the school, which became Studley College and continued until 1969. During the first decade of the 20th century, ladies from the college were already securing demanding positions as professional gardeners:

> '…I have six men under me, and a man from the estate to do the mowing, carting etc…there is a very pretty Italian garden, sub tropical beds, lily ponds, fern houses and several herbaceous borders in the kitchen garden, large lawns, seventy two vases to keep watered, strawberries etc…a small French garden…'
>
> Miss Lousada, *Studley Guild Magazine*, 1911

Studley graduates joined girls who had trained at other women's horticultural colleges, most notably Swanley College in Kent, which was established in 1889 and later became part of Wye College. Frances Wolseley founded Glynde School for Lady Gardeners in 1902, which recruited girls from middle-class families. In some cases their commitment to gardening and outdoor work was not all Wolseley hoped for:

> The students were told to begin work in the garden at 7a.m…they wore skirts for their first day's work, new sailor hats, short coats and skirts; the voiceless one had a fur boa round her neck: Dodd had not discarded her pearl necklace.

In 1895 another avenue opened to women who sought a serious career in horticulture, when the Director of Kew, Sir William Thistleton-Dyer, allowed girls to begin training in the botanic gardens. Their dress – thick brown bloomers with woollen stockings, fitted jackets and caps – caused great controversy and even inspired verse:

> They gardened in bloomers, the newspapers said,
> And so to Kew without waiting the Londoners sped;
> From the tops of the buses they had a fine view
> Of the ladies in bloomers who gardened at Kew.

Top: *A pruning lesson at Studley College, c1910. Below:* *Pupils at Westbourne school, Sheffield, 1903*

Plant hunting and plant introductions

By the end of the 19th century, plant hunting was big business. Large commercial nurseries were commissioning plant hunters to find new specimens for propagation and sale and The Royal Botanic Garden in Kew was overseeing the movement of plants throughout the Empire. Plants were arriving in Britain from countries as diverse as India, Australia, South Africa and South America as well as the USA, and specimens were beginning to trickle through from China and Japan, whetting Britain's horticultural appetite for South-East Asian plants. Continuing advances in international travel, communications and horticultural technology meant the 20th century promised to be an exciting time for plant hunters.

The period produced many detailed records of plant hunting expeditions. It was a time when professional horticulturalists and botanists were travelling to extreme parts of the world and the importance of recording information about native habitats and local conditions was appreciated. Many Asian plants bear the name of the plant hunters who first introduced them into western cultivation: 'wilsonii', 'forrestii', and 'farrerii' being familiar to many gardeners. Remarkably, the work of the plant hunters continued throughout the First World War, with expeditions still taking place throughout Asia, although the war took its horticultural toll in a different way; many of the plants collected by George Forrest and William

Bell flower, Campanula persicifolia

Purdom between 1914 and 1916 failed to survive on their arrival at Kew, due to a shortage of gardeners who were by then serving in the armed forces.

One of the many great plant hunters associated with this period is Ernest Henry Wilson (1876–1930), who was commissioned by the Veitch Nursery in London to travel to China in 1899 with a very specific brief: to collect the seed of *Davidia involucrate*, the handkerchief tree. After a perilous journey and several major set backs – including arriving at the known site of a *Davidia* only to discover it had recently been felled – Wilson found a tree in full bloom. The seed he collected on that journey was to produce 13,000 seedlings. Throughout his career Wilson collected almost 65,000 plants, including the regal lily, *Lilium regale*, and the seed of the blue plumbago, *Ceratostigma willmottiae*; this he sent to Ellen Willmott who had provided financial support for that particular expedition.

George Forrest (1873–1932) also ventured into China in search of new species and he took the innovative step of inviting owners of large private gardens to fund his trips in return for being a beneficiary of the collected material. Caerhays Castle in Cornwall was one of his sponsor gardens. Forrest's other ingenious idea was to train local people to collect from the Chinese provinces, which made an enormous

pool of experience and knowledge available to him. Well-known Forrest introductions include the large-leaved *Rhododendron sinogrande*, the shrub *Pieris formosa* var *forrestii*, a bluish-violet primula, *Primula vialii* and the blue-flowered alpine, *Gentiana sino-ornata*.

Reginald Farrer (1880–1920) was a specialist alpine plant collector who became one of the most influential names in rock gardening. His books, *My Rock Garden* (1907) and *The English Rock Garden* (1919), encouraged the fashion for these features in Britain. His approach was to mimic the plants' natural environment, placing rocks with their largest surface to the ground, with breaks in the lines of rock contrived to imitate natural faults.

Edward Augustus Bowles, an amateur collector, was a friend and travelling companion of Farrer's who introduced many fine plants. His books *My Garden in Spring*, *My Garden in Summer* and *My Garden in Autumn and Winter* describe the fine plant collection that he developed at his Enfield home, Myddleton House, in the early 20th century. Bowles was typical of an Edwardian gentleman, comfortably well off and with no need of professional employment, but with the skills, knowledge and time to commit to horticultural research.

Frank Kingdon Ward (1885–1958) is often referred to as the 'Blue Poppy Man' after his discovery on the Chinese/Tibetan border of the temperamental and elusive *Meconopsis betonicifolia* that still causes such excitement today. He and his second wife also braved an enormous earthquake that killed over a thousand people in Assam, to discover the exquisite cream-flowered shrub *Cornus kousa* var *chinensis*.

Clarence Elliot (1881–1969) carried out much of his plant-hunting closer to home, mostly in the Mediterranean, though in later years he also travelled to the Falkland Islands and South America. Our spring gardens would not be the same without the lime-green flowers of the hellebore Elliot introduced from Corsica: *Helleborus lividus corsicus*, now known as *Helleborus argutifolius*.

The blue poppy, Meconopsis betonicifolia

Like the hellebore, many of the plants we consider common in our gardens today were introduced or bred here during the Edwardian years. Rhododendrons are a fine example of a plant species that has made an enormous impact on British gardens and the range available expanded throughout the Edwardian period as Asian plant introductions increased. The now much-maligned *Rhododendron ponticum* was introduced in the 18th century and North American specimens had arrived in the early 19th century, but once the exquisite South-East Asian forms were seen they became the 'must have' plants of the time. In parts of Britain like the West Country, where the climate and conditions best mimicked their natural habitat, rhododendrons were grown in huge collections where their colours vied for attention each spring. The Hampshire garden of Exbury, Wakehurst Place in Sussex,

Rhododendrons at Exbury Gardens, Hampshire

John Waterer (right) in the Knaphill Nurseries, Woking, 1904

Bodnant, North Wales and Cragside in Northumberland still hold original Edwardian collections of rhododendrons. Rhododendron breeder John Waterer sent plants all over the world from his nursery at Knaphill near Woking; he even supplied the gardens of the White House in Washington DC.

These Edwardian plants typify the best in classic planting styles and combinations, as much as Edwardian gardens themselves epitomise the traditional English country garden. The richness of our gardens today owes much to the range and variety of plants that became available to British gardeners during the late Victorian and Edwardian periods.

GODETIA,
SUTTON'S DOUBLE ROSE.

Messrs
Sutton
acknowledge
with best
thanks the
valued order
just received,
which is having
their immediate attention.

The Royal Seed Establishment,
Reading.

Plant lists

The following lists of plants, while not exhaustive, give an indication of plants that were popular in Edwardian Britain. All the plants listed are available in one form or another, whether as seed, container-grown plants or in the case of some woodier plants, as bare rooted trees and shrubs. As many of the plants will have a range of modern hybrids, it is important to decide whether your planting must be authentic or whether it is to be 'in the style of' Edwardian planting, in which case you will have a wider palette to select from and will find the plants easier to obtain.

Many cultivated forms of plants will only be available as container-grown specimens because they are propagated vegetatively, as cuttings for example, rather than from seed. Some plants in the lists grow as wild flowers in the British Isles. It may be difficult to purchase some of these as container-grown species, as nurseries do not often propagate plants that commonly occur naturally as wildflowers or weeds in gardens, so seed may be your only option.

Please remember that under the Wildlife and Countryside Act it is illegal to uproot any wild plant and to take material from protected species. All the plants listed in this book are available from legitimate sources.

Postcard acknowledgement of order from Messrs Suttons, dated 1907

Plants Available  Widely available **Seed**  Available Widely available

Unusual Unusual

BOTANICAL NAME	COMMON NAME	PLANTS	SEED
Bulbs			
Allium cyaneum	Dark blue garlic		
Eucomis pallidiflora	Giant pineapple flower		
Galanthus reginae-olgae	Autumn snowdrop		
Lilium pardalinum	Leopard lily		
Lilium regale	Regal lily		
Lilium speciosum var gloriosoides			
Muscari botryoides	Baby's breath		
Tulipa kaufmanniana	Water lily tulip		
Hardy perennials & annuals			
Alstroemeria pelegrina 'Alba'	White lily of the Incas		
Anemone hupehensis	Chinese anemone		
Ceratostigma willmottianum	Chinese plumbago		
Corydalis scouleri			
Dicentra macrantha			
Gentiana farreri			
Gentiana sino-ornata	Showy Chinese gentian		
Helleborus argutifolius	Holly-leaved hellebore		
Heuchera sanguinea	Coral bells		
Hosta sieboldiana			
Linum narbonense	Blue flax		
Meconopsis delavayi			
Nemesia strumosa			
Papaver rhoeas Shirley group			
Phlox divaricata subsp *laphamii*	Wild sweet William		

BOTANICAL NAME	COMMON NAME	PLANTS	SEED
Primula forrestii		🌱	🟩
Primula rosea	Rosy primrose	🌱	🟩
Primula vialii	Vial's primrose	🌱 🌱	🟩 🟩
Ranunculus lyallii	Giant buttercup	🌱	🟩

Shrubs

Cornus kousa	Kousa	🌱	🟩
Enkianthus campanulatus	Redvein Enkianthus	🌱 🌱	🟩
Hamamelis mollis	Chinese witch hazel	🌱	🟩
Hebe cupressoides		🌱	🟩
Hebe odora		🌱	🟩
Hydrangea macrophylla 'Mariesii'	Hydrangea 'Mariesii'	🌱	🟫
Hydrangea macrophylla 'Veitchii'	Hydrangea 'Veitchii'	🌱	🟫
Olearia avicenniifolia		🌱	🟩
Olearia macrodonta	New Zealand holly	🌱 🌱	🟩
Olearia traversii	Ake-ake	🌱	🟩
Philadelphus microphyllus		🌱	🟩
Pieris formosa var forrestii		🌱	🟫
Pyracantha angustifolia		🌱	🟩
Rhododendron sinogrande	Great Chinese rhododendron	🌱	🟩
Rhus potaninii		🌱	🟩
Rosa 'Dorothy Perkins'		🌱	🟫
Rosa moyesii		🌱	🟩
Viburnum carlesii		🌱	🟩

Climbers

Actinidia deliciosa	Kiwi fruit	🌱	🟩

BOTANICAL NAME	COMMON NAME	PLANTS	SEED
Actinidia kolomikta	Kolomikta		
Fallopia baldschuanica	Russian vine		
Vitis coignetiae	Crimson glory vine		

Trees

Abies sachalinensis	Sakhalin fir		
Abies veitchii	Veitch fir		
x Cupressocyparis leylandii	Leyland cypress		
Davidia involucrata	Handkerchief tree		
Magnolia delavayi	Delavay's magnolia		

Gertrude Jekyll plants

Tender plants

Begonia metallica	Metal-leaf begonia		
Canna indica	Arrowroot		
Hibiscus rosa-sinensis	Blacking plant		
Passiflora racemosa	Red passion flower		

Bulbs

Chionodoxa luciliae	Glory of the snow		
Chionodoxa luciliae Gigantea group			
Corydalis cava	Holewort		
Erythronium dens-canis	Dog's tooth violet		
Iris 'Florentina'	Florentine iris		
Iris foetidissima	Stinking iris		
Iris reticulata	Early bulbous iris		
Iris unguicularis	Algerian iris		

BOTANICAL NAME	COMMON NAME	PLANTS	SEED
Leucojum vernum	Spring snowflake	🌱	🟩
Lilium auratum	Golden-rayed lily of Japan	🌱	🟩
Lilium lancifolium	Tiger lily	🌱	🟩
Lilium longiflorum	Bermuda lily	🌱	Cultivars available
Narcissus bulbocodium	Hoop petticoat daffodil	🌱	🟩
Ornithogalum nutans	Drooping star of Bethlehem	🌱	🟫
Puschkinia scilloides	Striped squill	🌱	🟩
Scilla bifolia	Alpine squill	🌱	🟩
Scilla sibirica	Siberian squill	🌱	🟩

For in and at the base of walls

Antirrhinum majus	Greater snapdragon	🌱	🟩
Campanula portenschlagiana	Wall bellflower	🌱 🌱	🟩
Cerastium tomentosum	Dusty miller	🌱	🟩
Digitalis purpurea f albiflora	White flowered foxglove	🌱 🌱	🟩
Erinus alpinus	Alpine balsam	🌱	🟩
Iris unguicularis	Algerian iris	🌱 🌱	🟩
Phlox x procumbens		🌱	🟫
Saxifraga umbrosa	True London pride	🌱	🟩

Perennials & annuals

Aster divaricatus		🌱 🌱	🟩
Bergenia cordifolia 'Purpurea'	Elephant ear 'Purpurea'	🌱	🟩
Campanula isophylla 'Alba'	Italian bellflower 'alba'	🌱	🟩
Euphorbia characias subsp Wulfenii	Mediterranean spurge	🌱 🌱	🟩
Gaultheria shallon	Salal	🌱	🟩
Gentiana asclepiadea	Willow gentian	🌱 🌱	🟩

BOTANICAL NAME	COMMON NAME	PLANTS	SEED
Heuchera richardsonii		🌱	🟩
Nigella damascena	Love-in-a-mist	🌱	🟩 🟩
Perovskia atriplicifolia	Russian sage	🌱	🟩
Primula florindae	Giant cowslip	🌱 🌱	🟩
Stachys byzantina	Lamb's ear	🌱 🌱	🟩 🟩
Veronica prostrate	Prostrate speedwell	🌱	🟩

Shrubs

Brachyglottis greyi		🌱	🟩
Buxus sempervirens	Common box	🌱 🌱	🟩
Cornus Canadensis	Creeping dogwood	🌱 🌱	🟩
Daphne mezereum	Mezereon	🌱 🌱	🟩
Leucothoe axillaries		🌱	🟩
Ligustrum ovalifolium 'Aureum'	Golden privet	🌱 🌱	🟫
Rhododendron ferrugineum	Alpenrose	🌱	🟩
Rhododendron 'Praecox'	Rhododendron 'Praecox'	🌱	🟫
Taxus baccata	English yew	🌱 🌱	🟩
Yucca recurvifolia	Curved-leaved spanish dagger	🌱	🟫

Climbers & wall plants

Abutilon vitifolium	Chilean tree mallow	🌱	🟩
Campsis radicans	Trumpet vine	🌱	🟩
Clematis flammula	Sweet-scented virgin's bower	🌱 🌱	🟩
Clematis montana	Mountain clematis	🌱	🟩
Clematis paniculata		🌱	🟩
Clematis vitalba	Traveller's joy	🌱	🟩
Clematis viticella	Purple clematis	🌱	🟩

BOTANICAL NAME	COMMON NAME	PLANTS	SEED
Solanum crispum	Potato tree	🪴	📦
Solanum laxum	Potato vine	🪴	📦
Vitis coignetiae	Crimson glory vine	🪴🪴	📦
Wisteria sinensis	Chinese wisteria	🪴🪴	📦

Old garden roses

Rosa arvensis	Field rose	🪴	📦
Rosa x centifolia	Cabbage rose	🪴	📦
Rosa x centifolia 'De Meaux'	Rose 'De Meaux'	🪴	📦
Rosa gallica 'Versicolor'	Rosa mundi	🪴	📦
Rosa 'Maiden's Blush'	Rose 'Maiden's Blush'	🪴	📦
Rosa 'Rose du Roi'	Rose 'Rose du Roi'	🪴	📦
Rosa rubiginosa	Eglantine	🪴	📦

Climbers & ramblers

Rosa banksiae	Banksian rose	🪴	📦
Rosa sempervirens	Evergreen rose	🪴	📦
Rosa 'Félicité Perpétue'	Rose 'Félicité Perpétue'	🪴	📦
Rosa laevigata	Cherokee rose	🪴	📦
Rosa moschata	Musk rose	🪴	📦

Pillar roses

Rosa 'Aimée Vibert'	Rose 'Aimée Vibert'	🪴	📦
Rosa 'Blairii Number Two'	Rose 'Blairii Number Two'	🪴	📦
Rosa 'Gloire de Dijon'	Old glory rose	🪴🪴	📦
Rosa 'Madame Alfred Carrière'	Rose 'Madame Alfred Carrière'	🪴	📦

BOTANICAL NAME	COMMON NAME	PLANTS	SEED

William Robinson plants

Hardy bulbs & tuberous plants

BOTANICAL NAME	COMMON NAME	PLANTS	SEED
Agapanthus campanulatus			
Allium azureum	Azure-flowered garlic		
Allium carinatum subsp pulchellum	Keeled garlic		
Allium moly	Golden-flowered garlic		
Allium neapolitanum	Daffodil garlic		
Allium triquetrum	Triquetrous leek		
Alstroemeria aurea	Peruvian lily		
Anemone blanda	Winter windflower		
Anemone coronaria	Garden anemone	Cultivars available	Cultivars available
Anthericum liliago	St Bernard's lily		
Colchicum autumnale	Meadow saffron		
Colchicum speciosum	Giant meadow saffron		
Convallaria majalis	Lily of the valley		
Crocosmia x crocosmiiflora	Montbretia		
Crocus biflorus	Cloth-of-silver		
Crocus chrysanthus	Crocus	Cultivars available	Cultivars available
Crocus flavus subsp flavus	Yellow crocus		
Crocus laevigatus	Smooth crocus		
Crocus speciosus	Large autumn crocus		
Fritillaria imperialis	Crown imperial		
Fritillaria meleagris	Snake's head fritillary		
Galanthus elwesii	Elwes's snowdrop		
Galanthus fosteri			

BOTANICAL NAME	COMMON NAME	PLANTS	SEED
Galanthus ikariae		🪴	◆
Galanthus nivalis subsp Imperati		🪴	▨
Galanthus plicatus	Crimean snowdrop	🪴	◆
Galtonia candicans	Summer hyacinth	🪴 🪴	◆
Hyacinthoides hispanica	Spanish bluebell	🪴	◆
Hyacinthoides italica	Italian bluebell	🪴	◆
Hyacinthoides non-scripta	Bluebell	🪴	◆
Iris delavayi	Delavay iris	🪴	◆
Iris germanica	Bearded iris	🪴	◆
Iris histrioides		🪴	◆
Iris pallida	Dalmatian iris	🪴	◆
Iris sibirica	Siberian flag	🪴	◆
Lilium auratum	Golden-rayed lily of Japan	🪴	◆
Lilium bulbiferum	Orange lily	🪴	◆
Lilium canadense	American meadow lily	🪴	◆
Lilium candidum	Madonna lily	🪴	◆
Lilium henryi	Henry's lily	🪴	◆
Lilium japonicum	Bamboo lily	🪴	▨
Muscari armeniacum	Armenian grape hyacinth	🪴	Cultivars available
Muscari botryoides	Baby's breath	🪴	▨
Muscari comosum	Tassel hyacinth	🪴	◆
Muscari neglectum	Common grape hyacinth	🪴	◆
Narcissus cyclamineus	Cyclamen-flowered daffodil	🪴	◆
Narcissus jonquilla	Jonquil	🪴	◆
Narcissus poeticus	Pheasant's eye	🪴	◆

BOTANICAL NAME	COMMON NAME	PLANTS	SEED
Narcissus pseudonarcissus	Wild daffodil	🌱	▨
Narcissus x odorus	Campernelle	🌱	▨
Pulsatilla alpine	Alpine anemone	🌱	▨
Ranunculus constantinopolitanus 'Plenus'		🌱	▨
Ranunculus crenatus		🌱	▨
Ranunculus glacialis		🌱	▨
Schizostylis coccinea	Crimson flag lily	🌱 🌱	▨
Scilla bifolia	Alpine squill	🌱	▨
Scilla sibirica	Siberian squill	🌱	▨
Trillium grandiflorum	American wake-robin	🌱 🌱	▨
Tulipa greigii	Greig's tulip	🌱	▨
Tulipa kaufmanniana	Water lily tulip	🌱	▨
Tulipa praestans		🌱	▨
Tulipa sylvestris	Wild tulip	🌱	▨

Climbing and wall plants

Abutilon vitifolium	Chilean tree mallow	🌱	▨
Akebia quinata	Chocolate vine	🌱 🌱	▨
Carpenteria californica	Tree anemone	🌱	▨
Ceanothus americanus	Indian tea	🌱	▨
Ceanothus cuneatus var *rigidus*	Monterey ceanothus	🌱	▨
Ceanothus dentatus	Tooth-leaved blue bush	🌱	▨
Clematis alpina	Austrian clematis	🌱	▨
Clematis armandii	Armand clematis	🌱 🌱	▨
Clematis cirrhosa	Evergreen clematis	🌱	▨
Clematis montana	Mountain clematis	🌱	▨

American wake-robin, Trillium grandiflorum

BOTANICAL NAME	COMMON NAME	PLANTS	SEED
Clematis orientalis	Oriental clematis	🪴	◆
Eccremocarpus scaber	Chilean glory flower	🪴	◆
Garrya elliptica	Silk tassel bush	🪴	◆
Hedera helix	Common ivy	🪴	◆
Indigofera heterantha	Himalayan indigo	🪴 🪴	◆
Jasminum humile	Italian yellow jasmine	🪴	◆
Jasminum nudiflorum	Winter jasmine	🪴 🪴	◆
Jasminum officinale	Common jasmine	🪴 🪴	◆
Lonicera japonica	Japanese honeysuckle	🪴	◆
Lonicera periclymenum	Common honeysuckle	🪴	◆
Lonicera sempervirens	Trumpet honeysuckle	🪴	◆
Parthenocissus henryana	Silver-vein creeper	🪴 🪴	◆
Parthenocissus quinquefolia	Virginia creeper	🪴 🪴	◆
Passiflora caerulea	Blue passion flower	🪴 🪴	◆ ◆
Rosa 'American Pillar'	Rose 'American Pillar'	🪴	◆
Rosa moschata	Musk rose	🪴	◆
Rosa 'Paul's Scarlet Climber'	Rose 'Paul's Scarlet Climber'	🪴	◆
Schizophragma hydrangeoides	Japanese hydrangea vine	🪴 🪴	◆
Vitis coignetiae	Crimson glory vine	🪴 🪴	◆
Vitis vinifera	Grape vine	🪴	◆
Wisteria brachybotrys		🪴	◆
Wisteria floribunda 'Multijuga'	Japanese wisteria 'Multijuga'	🪴 🪴	◆
Wisteria frutescens	American kidney bean tree	🪴	◆
Wisteria sinensis	Chinese wisteria	🪴 🪴	◆

BOTANICAL NAME	COMMON NAME	PLANTS	SEED
Plants for the wild garden			
Acanthus hungaricus	Long-leaved bears' breeches	🪴🪴	◆
Acanthus mollis	Bears' breeches	🪴🪴	◆
Acanthus spinosus Spinosissimus group		🪴	◆
Aconitum napellus	Monkshood	🪴🪴	◆
Aquilegia alpina	Alpine columbine	🪴	◆
Aquilegia canadensis	Akaly	🪴	◆ ◆
Aquilegia chrysantha	Golden-flowered columbine	🪴	◆
Aquilegia viridiflora		🪴	◆
Aquilegia vulgaris	Common columbine	🪴	◆ ◆
Campanula alpestris		🪴	◆
Campanula alpina	Alpine bellflower	🪴	◆
Campanula carpatica	American harebell	🪴	◆
Campanula glomerata	Clustered bellflower	🪴	◆
Campanula persicifolia	Fairy bellflower	🪴	◆
Campanula pyramidalis	Chimney bellflower	🪴	◆
Coronilla valentina subsp glauca	Glaucous scorpion-vetch	🪴	◆
Digitalis purpurea	Common foxglove	🪴	◆ ◆
Geranium cinereum	Ashy cranesbill	🪴	◆
Geranium endressii	Endres's cranesbill	🪴🪴	◆
Geranium psilostemon	Armenian cranesbill	🪴🪴	◆
Geranium sanguineum	Bloody cranesbill	🪴🪴	◆
Hemerocallis fulva	Common orange day lily	🪴	◆
Hemerocallis lilioasphodelus	Yellow day lily	🪴🪴	◆
Hippocrepis emerus	Scorpion senna	🪴	◆

BOTANICAL NAME	COMMON NAME	PLANTS	SEED
Hosta fortunei	Tall-cluster plantain lily		
Hosta lancifolia	Narrow-leaved plantain lily		
Hosta plantaginea var japonica	Japanese fragrant plantain lily		
Hosta sieboldii	Plantain lily		
Hypericum calycinum	Rose of Sharon		
Lunaria rediviva	Perennial honesty		
Polygonatum biflorum	Great solomon's seal		
Polygonatum hirtum			
Polygonatum multiflorum	Common solomon's seal		
Polygonatum odoratum	Angled solomon's seal		
Solidago flexicaulis			
Solidago odora	Blue mountain tea		
Solidago rigida			
Symphytum caucasicum	Caucasian comfrey		
Symphytum officinale	Common comfrey		
Thymus serpyllum	Wild thyme		
Trachystemon orientalis	Early-flowering borage		
Vinca major	Greater periwinkle		
Vinca minor	Lesser periwinkle		
Viola cornuta	Horned pansy		
Viola gracilis	Olympian violet		
Viola lutea	Mountain pansy		
Viola odorata	Sweet violet		

BOTANICAL NAME	COMMON NAME	PLANTS	SEED
Evergreen trees & shrubs			
Abies balsamea	Balsam fir		
Abies fraseri	Fraser's balsam fir		
Abies grandis	Grand fir		
Abies procera	Noble fir		
Araucaria araucana	Monkey puzzle		
Arbutus andrachne	Grecian strawberry tree		
Arbutus unedo	Strawberry tree		
Camellia reticulata cultivars	Netted camellia		
Choisya ternata	Mexican orange blossom		
Cistus crispus	Curled-leaved rock rose		
Cistus inflatus			
Cistus ladanifer	Common gum cistus		
Cistus x dansereaui			
Elaeagnus pungens	Silverthorn		
Escallonia rubra var macrantha	Chilean gum box		
Ilex crenata	Box-leaved holly		
Ilex latifolia	Tarajo holly		
Juniperus communis	Common juniper		
Juniperus recurva	Drooping juniper		
Juniperus rigida	Temple juniper		
Juniperus virginiana	Cedar oil tree		
Magnolia grandiflora	Bull bay		
Oleaira x haastii			
Olearia avicenniifolia			

BOTANICAL NAME	COMMON NAME	PLANTS	SEED
Phlomis fruticosa	Jerusalem sage	●●	◆
Phlomis tuberose	Sage-leaf mullein	●●	◆
Pinus mugo	Dwarf mountain pine	●	◆
Pinus nigra subsp *laricio*	Corsican pine	●	◆
Pinus radiate	Monterey pine	●	◆
Pinus sylvestris	Scots pine	●●	◆
Pinus wallichiana	Bhutan pine	●●	◆
Pleioblastus humilis	Toyooka-zasa	●	◇
Quercus acuta	Japanese evergreen oak	●	◆
Quercus ilex	Holm oak	●●	◆
Rhamnus alaternus var *augustifolia*		●	◇
Rhamnus californica		●	◆
Rhamnus cathartica	Purging buckthorn	●	◆
Rhododendron catawbiense	Mountain rosebay	●	◆
Rhododendron 'Catawbiense Grandiflorum'		●	◆
Rhododendron 'Mrs Lionel de Rothschild'	Rhododendron 'Mrs Lionel de Rothschild'	●	◇
Skimmia japonica		●	◆
Skimmia japonica 'Fragrans'	Skimmia 'Fragrans'	●	◇
Skimmia japonica 'Fragrantissima'		●	◇
Skimmia japonica subsp *Reevesiana*		●●	◇

Scoring system

Unusual = Not listed for sale in the *RHS Plant Finder* or *The Seed Search*

Available = available from up to 29 listed nurseries

Widely available = Available from over 30 listed nurseries

Edwardian Messenger's Conservatory

Further reading

Batey, Mavis and Lambert, David *The English Garden Tour*. London: John Murray, 1990

Brown, Jane *Lutyens and the Edwardians: An English Architect and His Clients*. London: Viking, 1996

Brown, Jane *Gardens of a Golden Afternoon*. London: Viking, 1982

Campbell-Culver, Maggie *The Origin of Plants*. London: Headline, 2001

Fearnley-Whittingstall, Jane *The Garden, An English Love Affair*. London: Weidenfeld & Nicholson, 2003

Hobhouse, *Penelope Plants in Garden History*. London: Pavilion, 1997

Jekyll, Gertrude *A Gardener's Testament*. Woodbridge: Antique Collector's Club, 1994

—- *Garden Ornament*. Woodbridge: Antique Collector's Club, 1994

—- *Colour in the Flower Garden*. RHS Classic garden writers series. London: Mitchell Beazley, 1995

Jekyll, Gertrude and Weaver, Lawrence *Arts and Crafts Gardens: Gardens for Small Country Houses*. Woodbridge: Garden Art Press, 1997

Robinson, William *The English Flower Garden*. Twickenham: Hamlyn, 1985

The RHS Plant Finder
Published annually by the Royal Horticultural Society, *the Plant Finder* lists more than 65,000 plants available from 800 nurseries as well as contact details, maps and opening hours for all the nurseries listed. There is also an online version of *the Plant Finder* on the RHS website: www.rhs.org.uk

The Seed Search
Now in its 5th edition, *The Seed Search* lists over 40,000 seeds available from 500 seed suppliers, with details of where to find them. It also includes 9,000 vegetable cultivars. Compiled and edited by Karen Platt, and online: www.seedsearch.demon.co.uk

*Opposite: **Frontispiece from Walter P Wright's** The New Gardening, 1912, showing yew topiary at Levens Hall, Cumbria*

Useful organisations and societies

The Museum of Garden History

The Museum of Garden History exists to enhance understanding and appreciation of the history and development of gardens and gardening in the UK., and was the world's first museum dedicated to this subject. Its attractions include a recreated 17th-century knot garden with historically authentic planting and collections of tools and gardening ephemera, as well as a well-stocked library.

www.museumgardenhistory.org

The Garden History Society

The Garden History Society aims to promote the study of the history of gardening, landscape gardens and horticulture, and to promote the protection and conservation of historic parks, gardens and designed landscapes and advise on their restoration. The Society runs a series of lectures, tours and events throughout the year.

www.gardenhistorysociety.org

The Royal Horticultural Society

The RHS is the world's leading horticultural organisation and the UK's leading gardening charity dedicated to advancing horticulture and promoting good gardening. It offers free horticultural advice and a seed service for its members and has plant centres at its four flagship gardens.

www.rhs.org.uk

The National Council for the Conservation of Plants and Gardens

The NCCPG seeks to conserve, document, promote and make available Britain and Ireland's garden plants for the benefit of horticulture, education and science. Its National Plant Collection scheme has 630 National Collections held in trust by private owners, specialist growers, arboreta, colleges, universities and botanic gardens.

www.nccpg.com

The Hardy Plant Society

With over 40 local groups in the UK, the Hardy Plant Society encourages interest in growing hardy perennial plants and provides members with information on both familiar and rarer perennial plants, how to grow them and where to find them. Its annual seed list is available for members to use and contribute to.

www.hardy-plant.org.uk

The Henry Doubleday Research Association

HDRA is a registered charity, and Europe's largest organic membership organisation. It is dedicated to researching and promoting organic gardening, farming and food. The HDRA's Heritage Seed Library saves hundreds of old and unusual vegetable varieties for posterity, also distributing them to its members. The HDRA currently manages the kitchen garden at Audley End, Essex, for English Heritage and runs Yalding Organic Gardens (see Places to visit).

www.hdra.org.uk

Centre for Organic Seed Information

Funded by DEFRA and run by the National Institute of Agricultural Botany and the Soil Association, the Centre for Organic Seed Information is a 'one-stop shop' for sourcing certified-organic seed from listed suppliers. It covers fruits, vegetables, grasses, herbs and ornamental plants among others.

www.cosi.org.uk

Local gardens trust and national plant societies

Almost all counties and regions of the UK have their own gardens trusts and most genera of plants have a national society. Your local groups may have fundraising plant sales or a members' seed list that you could join.

Places to visit

Athelhampton House
Athelhampton
Dorchester
Dorset
DT2 7LG
Tel: 01305 848363
E-mail: enquiry@athelhampton.co.uk
www.athelhampton.co.uk

Castle Ashby Gardens
Castle Ashby
Northamptonshire NN7 1LQ
Tel: 01604 696696
www.castleashby.co.uk

Cliveden
Maidenhead
Buckinghamshire SL6 0JA
Tel: 01628 605069
E-mail: cliveden@nationaltrust.org.uk
www.nationaltrust.org.uk

Easton Lodge
Little Easton
Great Dunmow
Essex CM6 2BB
Tel: 01371 876979
E-mail: enquiries@eastonlodge.co.uk
www.eastonlodge.co.uk

Eaton Hall
Eccleston
Chester
Cheshire CH4 9ET
Tel: 01244 684400
www.eeo.co.uk/grosvenor_estate/eaton_
gardens.asp

Godington Park
Ashford
Kent
TN23 3BW
Tel: 01233 620773
E-mail: ghpt@godington.fsnet.co.uk
www.gardenvisit.com/g/god2.htm

Graythwaite Hall
Newby Bridge
Ulverston
Hawkshead
Cumbria LA12 8BA
Tel: 015395 31333
www.visitcumbria.com/sl/grayhall.htm

Hatchlands Park
East Clandon
Guildford
Surrey GU4 7RT
Tel: 01483 222482
E-mail: hatchlands@nationaltrust.org.uk
www.nationaltrust.org.uk

Hestercombe Gardens
Cheddon Fitzpaine
Taunton
Somerset TA2 8LG
Tel: 01823 413923
www.hestercombegardens.com

Hidcote Manor Garden
Hidcote Bartrim
Nr Chipping Campden
GL52 6LR
Tel: 01386 438333
www.nationaltrust.org.uk/hidcote

Iford Manor
Bradford on Avon
Wiltshire
Tel: 01225 863146
www.ifordmanor.co.uk

Kelmscott Manor
Kelmscott
Lechlade
Gloucestershire GL7 3HJ
Tel: 01367 252486
E-mail: admin@kelmscottmanor.co.uk
www.kelmscottmanor.co.uk

Knebworth House
Knebworth
Hertfordshire SG3 6PY
Tel: 01438 812661
E-mail: info@knebworthhouse.com
www.knebworthhouse.com

Lindisfarne Castle
Holy Island
Berwick-upon-Tweed
Northumberland TD15 2SH
Tel: 01289 389244
E-mail: lindisfarne@nationaltrust.org.uk
www.nationaltrust.org.uk

Manor House Garden
Upton Grey
nr Basingstoke
Hampshire RG25 2RD
Tel: 01256 862827
E-mail: uptongrey.garden@lineone.net

Munstead Wood
Heath Lane
Godalming
Surry GU7 1UN
Tel: 01483 417867

Red House
Red House Lane
Bexleyheath
(Admission by pre-booked guided tour
only)
www.friends-red-house.co.uk

Renishaw Hall
Eckington
Sheffield
S21 3WB
Tel: 01246 432310
www.sitwell.co.uk

Shrubland Park
Coddenham
Ipswich
Suffolk IP6 9QQ
Tel: 01473 830221
E-mail: enquiries@shrublandpark.co.uk
www.shrublandpark.co.uk

Sulgrave Manor
Manor Road
Sulgrave
Banbury
Oxfordshire OX17 2SD
Tel: 01295 760205
E-mail: sulgrave-manor@talk21.com

Wightwick Manor
Wightwick Bank
Wolverhampton
West Midlands WV6 8EE
Tel: 01902 761400
E-mail:
wightwickmanor@nationaltrust.org.uk
www.nationaltrust.org.uk

Acknowledgements and picture credits

English Heritage and the Museum of Garden History would like to thank the many individuals who contributed to this volume, in particular Rowan Blaik for technical editing, James O Davies for photography and colleagues at the National Monuments Record for picture research. Thanks to Royal Botanic Gardens Kew for allowing access to the gardens for photography and to Livvy Gullen for further research.

The author would like to acknowledge the invaluable assistance of Jane Wilson, Fiona Hope and Philip Norman at the Museum of Garden History.

Unless otherwise stated, images are © English Heritage or © Crown copyright.NMR. All English Heritage photographs taken by James O Davies. Original artwork by Judith Dobie. Other illustrations reproduced by kind permission of:

The Art Archive: 65 (Royal Horticultural Society/Eileen Tweedy); Bridgeman Art Library: 12; Country Life Picture Library: 20, 35; Exbury Gardens: 66; Getty Images: 56–7; Jacques Amand: 4, 26, 33, 79; Mary Evans Picture Library: 6, 56; Museum of Garden History: facing p1, 2, 5, 7, 17, 22, 27, 28, 36, 38–9, 42, 45, 46, 48, 49, 50–2, 53, 54, 59, 67, 68, 85, 86, bc; National Portrait Gallery: 11 (NPGx6732), 23 (NPG D9486); Royal Botanic Gardens Edinburgh: 63.

Every effort has been made to trace copyright holders and we apologise in advance for any unintentional omissions or errors, which we would be pleased to correct in any subsequent edition of the book.

About the author

Anne Jennings is a freelance garden designer, consultant and writer, and Head of Horticulture at the Museum of Garden History. She is the co-author of *Knot Gardens and Parterres*, published by Barn Elms, and writes for a variety of gardening magazines.

Other titles in this series

Medieval Gardens

Georgian Gardens